Made in the USA
Thornton, CO
07/27/24 23:12:02

917f88f5-b402-4665-a3d9-b51a2cc050e9R01